Vampire Poetry

The Art of Breaking Down

ISBN 978-0-557-28533-4

© 2009 by Joel Collishaw All rights reserved.

"Black Butterfly"

Sometimes I look in the mirror
And hate everything I see
I look inside my eyes
And I just can't believe
I see so much dirt
Covering up the real me
So much sinful nature
I don't know how else to be

Sometimes it feels like
The whole world feels the same
Guilt has gotten the best of me
And all I feel is shame
On the outside I'm a rose
It's a radiant disguise
But the inside is stagnant
A notion I despise

It feels like I've been buried
I'm barely hanging on
People see me as a rock
But I'm not really that strong
I've been seeking change
But I'm stuck in the ground
Can't do this by myself

But I'm unlikely to be found

If one can be your rock
Explain the "rock bottom" theory
If I was in your shoes
I would not want to be near me
Would you fly with an eagle
That has never flown itself
Would you lean on me
Knowing you're all by yourself

Sometimes I pray
For the life of a butterfly
Beginning in a cocoon
I pray this beauty draws nigh
So I can leave the silky envelope
That retains the outer me
And morph into what
I'm destined to be

"The Evil One"

Can you so easily
Define a vampire and his heart
Or do you only know him
By the teeth that bare his mark

On the outside he is dark
But on the inside he is broken
For so long he has run
But tonight the truth shall be spoken

If you associate darkness with evil
And vampires fear light
Does that make him a devil
In your line of sight
Do you think his only goal
Is to break your precious heart
Or maybe it is you
He has feared from the very start

Two hearts that combine
Form a light that can be seen
But the light in which I fear
Exists within my queen
Like light, love is blinding
Leaving us in danger
So I distance myself
Remaining a total stranger

Garlic is the passion
That spreads throughout my veins
I enjoy the spice of love
But not as much as when it rains

There's risk in this venture
As it teases at my weakness
And you wonder why
I'm so quick to reside in meekness

You can see change in my eyes
In the presence of silver
Though I possess the key
I could never kill her
Silver is her power
To break any heart in two
Now tell me who's the evil one
Is it me or is it you

"Honest Demon"

I write with a question
Never having a goal to satisfy
So many questions revolve
Around one word, "why"
You read for answers
Or maybe something else
Hoping to find peace
In the pain I've endured myself

Does it reassure your broken heart

That life is not over
Since I have lived to tell
Refusing to be covert
I'll be the evil angel
Or the honest demon
But if you have dreams of me
I promise you'll wake up screaming

Tell me the roads of hell
That you have ventured through
I'll take you to deeper parts
Than you ever could construe
Show me the scars
You say you hide so well
Then I'll come out of the dark
So you can see how long I've been in hell

You'd think I was one of them
With "ugly" tattooed into my soul
Now leave this dark place
Before it swallows you whole
Pity and pain
Will eat the faith out of your skin
Leaving you dead inside
And hatred boiling within

Your eyes won't meet with mine

When I'm six feet below
With just an ounce of life left
I want hate-infested people to know
If you fall into a hole
And it's too dark for you to see
Don't dig down
It is not your destiny

"The Forgotten"

I exist all around you
Every place you go
Everywhere you look
I am there for you to know
Everything you hear
It's me right there
That frightful bitter feeling
With a cool brisk of air

It's me just being
Your worst memory
A nightmare, a haunting
In your precious little dream
Everything you wanted
That was bacteria to your soul
The love you once had

In the end I stole

If you want to forget
If you want to erase me
Close your eyes
Cause I'm everything you see
Close your ears
Cause I'm every song that you hear
The sound of the wind
Will bring back a hateful tear

Don't touch anything
That has a warming sensation
The touch will surely
Bring back all your frustration
Cut off all your senses
And then you can be happy
If any one is left undone
You will surely remember me

"The Rose"

Cursed from the beginning
Is the tunnel of my life
Anything that's good
Always leaves with time

Each time unprepared
As it catches me by surprise
And every time I shed
A tear from my eyes

The lonely road of faith
Is as narrow as it seems
Sometimes I forget
That I'm just a human being
As all good things pass
And hurt is inevitable
But as an emotional mind
I am blinded to the logical

Walking a straight path
On a plain dirt road
The storms that struck me
Were more than I was owed
But as life would have it
I come across a rose
Buried in my heart
And continuing to grow

A light of memories
Strike upon my mind
As I know that this rose
Will bring pain within time

The love and joy
That I experience in my walk
Takes me off my path
Flying over seas like a hawk

But life won't have it
That's why I have dreams
So that I can wish to the stars
That you will never leave
But I'll pray that just once
This rose will stay apart of me
Because I've felt a lot of pain
But this time I might bleed

"Garden of Love"

How can the world
Collapse at one time
Not the world around me
But the world in my mind
If things happen for a reason
Please tell me why
For so many times in confusion
I ran away to hide

Confusion hits me

Like the blind leading the blind
Whispers in the wind
Tell me I'm running out of time
How do I not do
The things I desire most
Like thorns resisting to grow
On the stem of a rose

Is the tree I seek
The forbidden one
"Seek not the tree
That hideth from the sun"
I see it in the dark
Shaded from the rest
But I see so much more
When all you see is less

Rotted love caused
By a lifetime of tears
Tolerance of emotion
Built up over the years
I ask you God
May I eat upon this tree
No one else knows
What it means to me

When all else is blind

I see true potential
Not loved by all
But to me is beyond special
Perhaps not the most
Perfect that you speak of
But it's all that I need
In the Garden of Love

"Love Her Better"

She's filled to the top
Like a glass of water
So far from home
And all she wants is her father
Her burdens weigh heavy
On such innocent hands
Even with this chain
She continues to stand

She's stronger then most
But she's fading away
The pressures of life
Are just too hard to sway
I've seen her tears
From heartache to heart break
Not that I wasn't to blame

I've made my mistakes

I would do anything
To reach down and save her
Take all of the pieces
And fix all that's been shattered
The look in her eyes
Say she's screaming so loud
I can hear her cry
Though she never makes a sound

But I know you love her
More then I ever could
I pray you take away the bad
And bless her with the good
Wrap your angel wings
Around her gracious soul
You can take pieces of me
Just make her feel whole

"Secret Island"

What is this feeling
I'm feeling inside
Like darkness has left
Suddenly I feel alive

I'm walking on a thin breeze
But I know you're there
And every time I fall
I know you still care

I don't know how you do
All the things you do
Every little thing
And I'm amazed by you
I'd say you're like an angel
Sent from above
But not even they
Could match all of your love

You truly are everything
That matters in my life
Like the world without stars
It just doesn't seem right
You make a silent stream
Out of crashing waves
And for all that I've done
You always forgave

So beautiful to me
Inside and out
You make life sound so sweet
When it seems so loud

You're essential to me
And the air I breathe
That small gust of wind
That always carries me

You're the sweet taste of love
That runs through my veins
Bringing colored emotion
On all my rainy days
I'm a body of water
As big as an ocean
But you're the secret little island
That gives me my emotion

"Sabotage"

For one reason or another
I rip roses out of the ground
Scream at the top of my lungs
When no one is making a sound
Paint gray on art
That has constructive colors
Exercising the right
To be different then all others

But why do I kill the rose

That has grown in my own yard
Taken away my silence
When my nights have been scarred
Why paint over beauty
That I have created myself
Why try to be different
When I'm unlike anyone else

I look for flaws in perfection
For it cannot exist
There's a devil near every angel
Just waiting to be missed
My obsession extracts me
Until I find the damage I desire
Like I thrive on being hurt
By putting myself in fire

Am I used to the pain
So I look for the knife
Do the tears I shed
Make me feel more alive
Why is it so hard to believe
That something can be perfect
If it doesn't come with pain
Then is it not worth it

Sabotage, is it simple

Are we ever fully aware
Or is it just me that thinks
No one really cares
And if I'm proven wrong
And love wraps its arms around me
Surely I'll push it away
Cause it's the only way I know how to be

"A Knife In His Heart"

In the beginning there was man
Caught in a plague of nature
Surviving mortality
Was an immoral transfer
Simplicity existed
In the core of a simple man
But the angels sought detail
On a heart soon to be damned

The king became weak
As he crawled in the dark
A storm passed through
As lightning struck a queen of hearts
He looked up to see a glow
Around a figure he'd never seen
Unwanted but adored

Were the elements of his queen

As the strings of his heart
Became tangled up in hers
His vision toward distance
Suddenly became a blur
He fell into her love
With a splash of risk and pain
Blinded by her love
He never saw danger in the rain

So tightly woven together
Their hearts appeared to be one
As time had drawn them closer
Regardless of what the other had done
Destiny played its part
Being the magnet in this game
Fate shares common interest
But often takes the blame

Mesmerized by her eye of deceit
He denied what was true
As she ventured out in boredom
To explore something new
The glow became dim
As he regained sight of reality
Anger built up inside

Brought on a foretold fatality

He saw her adulterous ways
In the bed in which they lay
Rage rolled in like thunder
But the words he would never say
In tears he looked over her
As she slept in his bed
He showed her how he felt
With a knife to her chest

"The Omen"

A pale moonlight kisses
Off the surface of her skin
Her eyes resemble the sky
With a dark blue trim
Her lips look gentle
Masking the monster inside
She said she'd never hurt me
But her promises turned to lies

Her hair blended in
With the darkness of the night
She cried as she left
Mumbling words of an internal fight

Confused of her nature
Only made me more intrigued
But the love I cast upon her
Only made her more fatigued

Wearing down the monster
That dwelled within her soul
Bringing tears to her eyes
Was like blood seeping out of coal
Living in a darkness
With no human compassion
Brought feelings of fear
To a place there never has been

She never tasted a tear
That had run down her face
Light shining in on her
Made her heart begin to race
Her weakness made her afraid
To live out in the open
Apart under the same moon
We wait for an omen

"In The Rain"

Hush Little Angel

Don't say a word
I know you never meant
To cause me any hurt
Don't think I've forgotten
About the love we shared
Don't think I forgot
How much you cared

We knew from the beginning
When we gave into each other
From that moment on
We would be together forever
If not in the physical
We'd always share our hearts
As hard as we may try
They cannot be taken apart

Hush Little Angel
Don't cry for my pain
I let go of your hand
To be alone in the rain
We both have cried
For the pain inside
But the love within
Has never died

Love is depicted

By the shape of your smile
But getting through the pain
Makes it all worth while
Tears are only a sign
That true love did exist
And how much it was worth
That we still took the risk

Hush Little Angel
I know the sound of your love
It whispers so softly
I'm the one you're thinking of
Just close your eyes
And concentrate on the pain
If all you see is my absence
Come join me in the rain

"Little Black Bird"

A little black bird
Torn to pieces inside
Weighed down by rocks
When all she wants is to fly
Yet I see a bright light
Shining from behind
A dark cloud moving west

And a light able to shine

Beat down by flaws
And let down by life
Barely able to see
The break of light
But outside the cave
She feels condemned to
Is a future with love
That God holds true

Little black bird
You're not frozen where you walk
God can hear your voice
When you feel you cannot talk
Little black bird
New chapters do exist
A couple of bad choices
Are nothing God can't fix

Little black bird
Not every dream comes true
But believe in God
For he has a plan for you
Little black bird
Don't give up when things are bad
Don't give up on yourself

No one else has

"The Vampire Inside Me"

The power seduces me
Like a secret addiction
Hiding in a glass bottle
Yet no one sees my affliction
They refer to them with fear
As vampires and witches
Alone I roam
With a bag full of glitches

My flaws precede me
Mirroring off into the light
Traveling at sonic speeds
With blood from my bite
Appealing to the lost eye
Looking for a path
Nowhere near my victim
Yet they fall into my wrath

A power I've attained
But never desired
Spreading my pain
Like a wild fire

My body serves as a cave
For a broken down spirit
Screams are apparent
For those who care to hear it

When all are asleep
And fully unaware
The night is my playground
In my state of despair
Responsibility of power
Makes temptation intense
Knowing someone is watching
With the possibility of influence

"The Mask"

Shadowing my mystery
With a mask and its glare
Revealing nothing
Of which you wouldn't care
Setting up an illusion
Only for you to see
Confidence and pride
To formulate my dream

Lies over lies

Infatuated with my own envy and lust
Creating my fate as I see it
Excluding anything not just
Playing life like a game
Only with my highest cards
Sometimes I wonder
If it's getting me very far

Fear of failure
And falling too deep
I'll mask my reality
For only my keep
And at the end of the night
I'll still be alone
As a mirror reflects my image
And the truth still be shown

Admitting I fear
That I'm not all that you desire
Without my mask
Reveals a wrath of fire
In the shadows I stand
Only flesh and blood
Knowing in this skin
That you could never love

Like a perfect storm

For one that wears the mask of disguise
He is blind to all of creation
Behind blue eyes
Coving up the truth
And all of my past
The protection to my soul
…The Mask

"Dirt"

A God given life
I am one of the Sheppard's lambs
But I'm not happy with this life
Not happy with who I am
I could be anything else
Just take away my soul
Take away my heart
And replace it with coal

Make me a rose
With no meaning of emotion
Not the shark that must feed
And rule all of the ocean
Like the king of the jungle
We as humans must succeed
Where as I like a withered rose

Would rather recede

Make me a rock
That feels nothing at all
There's no pain in slipping
No matter how far the fall
Or something of the desert
Dry like the sand
No rain drops of failure
To show how miserable I am

Pour your rain on me
And mix it like mud
Evaporate my misery
So I can see it rise up
Reverse my creation
To the way I began
Turn me back to dust
That's as valued as I am

Dirt as I started
And dirt I shall die
But if I'm never gonna be happy
Then why live this life
I don't wanna live
Feeling so hurt
Reverse my creation

And put me back into the dirt

"The Book"

I feel like a closed book
The way I hide everything inside
Looking at the cover
It appears to be normal but the title's a lie
I fit in with everyone
Just another book on the shelf
But if you read the pages of my life
You'd see something else

I thought I could control all these feelings
With the words I write
Organizing by chapter
To help this weary mind sleep at night
But half the pages are blank
Cause I can never get it out
And the rest are just words
No one cares to figure out

I could write a thousand pages
And still not empty these emotions
Filled with hurt combined with passion
Yet I just go through the motions

The words might not make sense
But it's everything from inside of me
I'm a closed book waiting
For someone to want to read

"Your Kiss"

Remember me
From the past
I used to be
Like broken glass
Remember how
You glued each piece
But look at me now
What's happened to me

I sleep all day
So I can dream
I hear you say
You still care for me
In your eyes
I see a smile
But they're all lies
I'm in denial

So I'll dance off

To an isle of betrayal
Your new love
Doesn't care how I feel
And I understand
No one wants to live in the past
But I thought, "I love you"
Meant something would last

Knowing what I know
I feel so helpless
Can't escape the dark
Knowing your someone else's
So I'll sleep forever
In a coffin of bliss
Like a vampire
I'll have to dream of your kiss

"Taking a Bullet"

No one can say that
I have never loved
For I still pray
For the one I let go
No one can say
That I love so easy
Because there is only one

For which it shows

My presence no longer
Lets the eye see
Nor my voice
Whisper the words
But good intention
And sacrifice
Now have you
Singing like a bird

No one can say that
My love was not real
For it has not found
A new resting place
And no one can say
I made a mistake
Because my pain is worth
The smile on your face

"And Love Said No"

I want to know
What all of this is
I've been through ups and downs
But nothing like this

Emotion of the heart
Flowing like lava to my brain
Fueling my heart
But it doesn't feel the same

I want to know how it entered
Through a thickened stream
I've been guarded all along
Like war heroes and their dream
Slashed through like a knife
It's been daggered into my soul
I feel the burning and twisting
Creating a deeper hole

I can feel my cold heart
And the warmth of your love
I look down in disgust
But grin to the above
Though it's all been introduced
And it's still so new
Now I must ask
What is this feeling I have for you

I want to know what you call
This powerful warmth
This overwhelming emotion
I wish to call forth

I say to you now
So that everyone might know
"Is it you that I'm feeling"
And love said, "No"

"If Only in My Mind"

Just a young man
With a handful of dreams
Knowing that life
Isn't all that it seems
Questions of fate
And the road to destiny
I feel like I'm screaming
But no one is listening

Drifting in the current
As if I have no place to go
Just waiting for life
Going with the flow
What is fate
What will life have of me
And if I'm blinded by fear
Then how can I see

Just a small child

In the eyes of Christ
With a longing of greatness
And mapped out life
What it is I don't know
For all I see is a blank sheet
I'm locked in a darkness
For which I cannot possess the key

A poor boy
With diminished schemes
A hopeless heart
And broken dreams
I desire more
Than this life has had to offer
Not the simple ways of land
But rather the ways of water

The risks, the chances
And the consequences I would take
Just to fill this void of wanting
To be something great
To leave a small set of footprints
In the sands of time
To know I was worth something
If only in my mind

"Confessions of a Sinner"

Father God in Heaven
I pour out my soul
A confession of my sins
I pray you can fill the holes
My heart is black
And I've destroyed this temple
They say you forgive
But is it really that simple

I've lied a thousand times
And even denied your name
Stole what wasn't mine
And let someone else take the blame
I've cursed to the stars
Blaming you for my mistakes
Smoke cigarettes to relieve the stress
And weed when it's too much to take

I've tried to drink away my sorrows
But they only progressed
Devoured enough cocaine
To get me through times of distress
Doing everything and anything
To escape this reality
Not once considering

My actions turning into fatality

So tell me is it easy
To forgive someone like me
I know that you care
Though sometimes I can't see
I've tried everything I can
I've got nowhere else to turn
Lord, save me from myself
Before the devil in me returns

"Shining Star"

Every dark day
Has a shining star
You can spot it easily
Even when it seems too far
There's no doubt in my mind
That you are that star
Cause I love you for you
And not what you are

I wait all night
To see you shine
And when I do
It makes me feel so alive

There's no bad day
With you by my side
And I know that our love
Will never die

It seems unreal
Like a fantasy dream
Everything is perfect
The way it should be
It doesn't matter
How we came to be
As long as you're here
Close with me

I'll never let go
And fade back to the dark
You've infused these feelings
Into my heart
If I didn't have you
I couldn't go far
I need my only love
My shining star

"Resurrected Love"

The death of my first love

Has left me alone and bitter
The days have been as cold
As the night's rainy weather
I've been thirsting for a hand
To reach out and touch my face
A new love to replace
The dust that's collected in this place

I've grown cold over the years
And my tears have turned to blood
The rain pours out my sadness
Creating a destructive flood
Though I miss the first love
That set fire in my heart
I feel a new sense of warmth
That has no plan to depart

She looks into my eyes
With innocence and confusion
Wondering why my skin crawls
Or if I've created an illusion
Why it looks like my skin
Is crumbling like concrete
She doesn't have a clue
My life has died inside of me

As her head lies on my chest

And her hand runs through my hair
I feel a sudden sense of warmth
And a change in the air
Like I've been chained under water
It feels like my first breath
Her love has brought me to life
When I've been living a life of death

The coolness of my skin
And the glare in my eye
Doesn't seem to faze her
Except for my attempts to say goodbye
My heart begins to replenish
With a fresh batch of blood
I fear this new beginning
But I'm resurrected by her love

"The Mask of Two Angels"

If seduction were an art
I'd paint your name inside angel wings
As you would build a sculpture
Of a queen without her king
Bullet casings outline
The lonely figure you've created
And the wall you've built

Has left your heart numb and sedated

You detest the conversion
Of lust into love
Beginning with merriment
Coercion, a solution thereof
To protect your heart of fragility
From the peril I possess
Yet you play with my fire
For the danger you obsess

Consciously aware
Of the halo you conceal
Melts the disguise I've maintained
To mask how I feel
I see fear bleeding from your eyes
As I uncover your innocence
Fear not my love
For I am an angel of suspense

Dressed in red and black
I'm not so different from you
The masks may differentiate
But we share the same view
Giving fear in the form of seduction
For those that lust a change
Then go back to the flawless

When they can't handle the deranged

Eroticism serves the sinful nature
Protecting us from pain
A peculiar approach
Yet deep down we are the same
As we share our love
We share the art that ended our war
Soon I'll burn the sculpture
As you blend my name with yours

"The Beautiful Letdown"

Walking for days
On the desert land
Just hoping for water
An oasis in the sand
I think I see it
A glimmer of fluid
My glare becomes intense
Nothing to taste, but I already knew it

Building a bridge
To find the other side
Half way across
I can see the ocean tide

Almost to shore
As my eyes slowly close
The bridge collapses
But I already know

The girl of all dreams
Has caught on to me
A true smile on my face
For everyone to see
But I can feel this one fading
It's been hanging around
But I already know
It's the beautiful letdown

"Attempted Murder"

For many years
I've been trying to kill a man
The reasons are unclear
For not even I understand
The tears trickle down my face
And gather on my lip
The taste is as bitter as I feel
Like a pirate and his ship

I've provoked this man

Into violence and anger
He knows me very well
For I am no stranger
His short temper and impatience
Gave me an upper hand
I could have had him in prison
But things didn't work out as planned

I've tricked him into drinking
Poison over and over
I've been his personal demon
Anything but a four-leaved clover
He's been too blind to see
What I've been trying to do
So pitiful that he believes
Everything I say is true

The impossible, a plan
I never thought I could attain
Murder through suicide
Something I could sustain
Deceit that would leave him
Injecting poison to his brain
Like a puppet on strings
I've gained control of this game

Though his body still lives

I've killed his spirit of hope
Feeling empty and unworthy
He still doesn't even know
For twenty some years
I've never even seen
The man I've been trying to kill
….Was me

"Who Am I"

How might one know
What life expects of thee
Who's to say the direction
Of our entire destiny
Everyone eagerly speaks of
Their own special path
So direct and specific
Like they're doing simple math

I stand alone in an empty space
As far as I can see
Feeling like this life
Has nothing in mind for me
What is this life
I don't understand
What am I supposed to do

What are its demands

As I sit alone
Listening for direction
Looking into a broken mirror
I can't see my own reflection
It seems like every person
Has a manual for their lives
A goal to where they're going
Something to which they strive

So I mumble a few words
With my last bit of hope
Looking for an answer
For all the questions I've wrote
I just wish I knew
What I was supposed to do
What value is the seed
That never even grew

"Misunderstood"

The cuts on her body
Surface blood to the skin
She intends to release her pain
From the dark places she has been

The razor draws blood
But in her eyes it draws peace
As it calms the storm in her mind
And puts her heart at ease

An expert of the mind
May conclude she be at risk
Suicidal tendencies
He's positive will persist
But without question
He never bothers to look inside
Only the scars on her body
Have told this story, a lie

You can see the hurt
With the depth of her tear
The scars inside
Run deeper than what you see here
Emotionally wounded
From the world spitting fire
And as she runs for help
The flames only get higher

Shape the cuts on her body
Into the words she feels
Her cry for help
Is as transparent as she conceals

The angel of death
Has not enticed her unto his world
She just wants someone to understand
A misunderstood girl

"Sentimentality of Nature"

When you look over the ocean
There's so much to be described
All the physical images
And the beauty that has derived
Nature brings peace
To the human heart
But brings out feeling
In the secret parts

Images created by God
Develop mental images in our mind
People search their hearts
Hoping to see what they can find
To see the water in a stream
Shimmer and flow with ease
Brings a sense of peace to the heart
And the mind to be relieved

And when you look up and see

The stars in the sky
It makes you appreciate
All the beautiful things you have in life
You start to realize
All that you've been blessed with
The things we take for granted
And always seem to forget

To love and be loved
Is a blessing of its own
The possibilities of life
Could leave you all alone
It's not the things you have in life
That are valued as important
It's who you have in your life
That keeps us from being dormant

The actions you take
And the things you say
Could impact someone's life
In many different ways
It doesn't matter what you say
For your love to be received
It's the things you do
That makes others believe

"Dark Side of the Ocean"

Whisper the screams
That rip through your mind
Open up like a book
And leave your fears behind
Your words are not words
They weave their way into my skin
Relieving you of treachery
And injecting me with him

Instinct has you gasping
For a breath of fresh air
You can't find the words
But I can see them in your stare
The quickness in your eye
Is asking a million questions
And the sparkle when they settle
Is pertinent to confessions

You have allowed this blade
To become embedded in your heart
Blinded by the fruits of lust
Which left you in the dark
How long will you allow
These hands to lead you to your demise
Black and blue are not your colors

When you have beautiful brown eyes

In the middle of the ocean
Under a blanket of darkness
The strength of the water
Seems to control us
But I'll be the candle
If you provide the flame
So many have given up
But you don't have to be the same

"In Lust and In Love"

The touch of your skin
Is all that I need
The tender feeling of your body
On top of me
An essential feeling
Like I'm apart of you
Ways of physical passion
Letting emotion shine through

I can feel your love
On the surface of my skin
As you grab me closer
To endure in a pleasurable sin

Not only a method
Of sexual delectation
But becoming more passionate
Than either of our expectations

As my hand slowly caress'
Your legs and thighs
I can see the felicity
Melting in your eyes
I want to show you
I can be everything you need
Show you with love
Nobody can treat you like me

I could never get enough
Of your luscious enchantment
Such a sexual vibe
While burning emotions are being sent
Lust and attraction
Take us to mountains of pleasure
But combining it with our passion
Makes for something you cannot measure

I'll love you down
Make you feel like a queen
I want to show you everyday
That you're everything I need

Make you so weak
You can't say a thing
Make you feel like no one
Can give you the things I bring

Nothing exceeds
Making love to the one you desire
The flames of emotion
Burning like fire
These feelings are unexplainable
Like nothing I could think of
You're everything I want
In lust and in love

"Wait For Each Other"

It's a gift from God
That I chose to abuse
Something I should have saved
For only you
Lust in my eye
Drew me to sin
Not knowing I'd regret
What I did back then

I'm filthy and dirty

Several times over
The shame hangs on my head
With the weight on my shoulder
Mother always said
It's better if you wait
I wish I could go back
But now it's too late

I gave up my body
To the devil for free
Taking advantage
Of the hopelessness inside of me
I wish I could go back
And wait for your love
Then I'd be giving myself
To an angel from above

Now I can see
Why abstinence is of value
The past makes me feel
Not good enough for you
Though we both have fallen
Into lust and its pleasure
I'll always wish
We would have waited for each other

"Divine"

What is this blue sky
That extends into forever
So beautiful from day to day
Somehow changing in its weather
Blue, orange, purple and red
Altering its color
Not only appearance
But what it does for another

Magically precipitating
Water rises to the air
Forming soft gray pillows
By the sun as it glares
On darker days
It gives back everything it stole
Feeding Mother Nature
And watering her soul

When the sun goes to rest
You can see all the eyes
Thousands of glares
Coming from a blackened sky
And a moon that looks down
As the night quietly sleeps
In different shapes

In the dark sky it creeps

The perfection of it all
To have always been
If it never started
Will it never end
But to argue with odds
That perfection comes with time
Perhaps then someone knew
The secret to creating the divine

"Cancer"

The ink on my left arm
Reminds me everyday
That miracles can happen
For those who pray
I too have felt alone
Looking for an answer
When a loved one grows sick
With leukemia, this cancer

Every prayer said
Builds up hope and faith
Every person who believes
Gives our loved one the strength

Keep praying and believing
For God is faithful
Even though the road
Might be rough and painful

I'm one of many
Though it seems so miniscule
Every little bit counts
Like a scarce type of jewel
Tonight I pray
For a boy I've never met
A miracle upon you
So that you shall never forget

All the people who cared
And a God who laid his touch
A blessing so precious
For he loved you this much
And I pray for the family
Believe in your prayers
Sometimes it doesn't seem it
But God really does care

"What Have I Become"

What have I become

Just another nobody
When all I really wanted
Was to be a somebody
I've come face to face
With my biggest fear
Not so much of failure
But what I feel is near

God has wasted his time
With my own creation
I'll disintegrate in the air
With at least a taste of salvation
If not I'll fade away
In the deepest crest of the earth
As I'll pray to the father
For a chance to start from birth

I don't know why
You put me here in the first place
You know I'd let you down
Only to see tears run down my face
If I had it my way
I'd rather have never been
I've hit rock bottom
I feel I can never win

Death seems much better

When faced with my thoughts
My dreams have gone to waste
As the rest of my mind rots
And all I really wanted
Was to be something great
Now I'm farther along
Seeing that it's probably too late

"Seeking Out Eve"

Don't fall for me
It's called falling for a reason
You think you can fly
Or at least that's what you're believing
Head over heals
That means you landed on your face
Don't take it that far
You know it's only a waste

They say falling in love
Can be the best emotion to have
But the fact remains
When you fall it ends up bad
No matter how far the fall
You will always get hurt
But you fell too hard

Even when I turned concrete to dirt

You thought I was pushing you
Far away from me
So you kept running back
Like I'd be enthused by your dreams
But I was pushing you away
From the edge of your fall
I just don't understand
Why you had to play around at all

God told Adam
Not to eat of this tree
For his own protection he listened
But you're seeking out eve
Do you enjoy the risk
Or do you think that I lie
You'll end up heartbroken
No matter how high

"Sea of Sorrow"

Part of me hates who I was
But I hate more of what I am
I'm letting my life slip
Like sand slips through your hands

It's so hard to win
And so easy to fail
I need something to believe in
Something that's real

I'm hanging by a thread
Because I still wanna believe
That there's a way out
Even though I can't see
I'm not worthy of Heaven
So inject my soul with fire
Make me a new man
So that one day I may inspire

I just wanna find
The better part of me
Heal all these wounds
Because I don't wanna bleed
I smother myself
With all of Satan's desires
Thinking it's what I wanted
But the devil is a liar

I'm tired of being
What he wants me to be
But is it too late
To change the dark side of me

If I could see God
I'd ask for another life to borrow
If only for a day
I could escape this sea of sorrow

"Tortured Soul"

A lonely man is me
So lost in sin
Walking in a darkness
Praying you'll let me in
I see a light
But that which seems too far
Draw me to this change
Away from an evil star

I walk this world alone
Roaming in a daze
Please help this soul
It seems to have lost its way
Stumbled has thee
So many times
Always pulled down
Before the positive could shine

Almost destined to be

In the flames of hell
May I ask for thy hand
For every time that I fell
Similar to thy walk
On water and ice
Save me from slipping
Into more pains and strife

Tortured is thy soul
But never to be the same
Label this black heart
As Oscuridad be thy name
God, help me out
Of this self created hell
It eats this weak body apart
Cell by cell

Soon there will be
Nothing left of thee
Maybe an overlook
Of where I should be
Please freeze the flames
That burn so many holes
Oh God, why do ye
Torture thy soul

"Sorry"

The bacteria in your heart
That was infecting your life
Twisting in your side
Like the sharpest part of a knife
A fatal virus, eating you
From the inside out
So how can you say
That I never caused you doubt

We laughed and cried together
While loved stained itself to our memory
Never to be forgotten
Was the lesson in love you left for me
You've painted me a picture
Complete with the frame
You're standing with innocence
Looking down at a ball and chain

I never meant to be
The weight that kept you from flying
You said things got better when I left
And you weren't even trying
I'm sorry for being the poison
That got you way off track
The negative influence I was

I guess I never realized any of that

Now I see I didn't leave
God took me away
So that you might have a chance
To have a brighter today
I always knew there was a reason
But I didn't know why
I guess things worked out
Because I was ruining your life

I hoped when you thought of me
You would always smile
Look at our love
Like it was all worthwhile
Now I can see purpose
In our painful goodbyes
I guess all I can do
Is apologize…

"War (Breaking Stone)"

Take my life
Or I'll take yours
I'll steal your nirvana
While you inherit my wars

Then I can walk
In your peaceful shoes
While you get to see
Things from my point of view

How do you like it
Does it hurt inside
When you feel my pain
Does it make you want to die
Do you feel it to the core
Deep inside your bones
Cause I built that heart
That you call a stone

Who am I to blame
I know it wasn't your fault
But I'm sure you have no problem
Taking my wounds and adding salt
The fire has been started
Let's fuel up the flames
Inviting devils to my life
Calling them out by name

I hate them
More than I hate you
But for some reason
I do what they want me to

I'm not as bad
As I sometimes seem
Perhaps you'd understand
If you understood my dreams

Yes I am the man
Who modified a genuine heart
Condensing and hardening
So it could not be torn apart
But pain is still gaining
As it fractures to the core
Turns out I was not prepared
For this type of war

"Playing with Satan"

Sleeping with the devil
I can feel the burn
Playing with my life
Like there's no concern
Young and naïve
As I jump into the deep end
Making my bad habits
A personal trend

I can swim for hours

In a pool of poison
As I ignore my constant
Voice of reason
Years have past
And I have no regrets
But I'm getting bored
I must admit

Surviving the deep end
There's more to explore
As I roam the forest
Searching for something more
Testing my limits
I breathe toxic waste
Little green plants
With a shot to the face

Lost in the forest
I've stumbled into snow
A new experience
As I feel the effects of Satan's blow
Windy and cold
But I just can't stray
As the wind touches my face
Numbing the pain away

Somehow I've lost myself

In the midst of my curiosity
Killing myself
In a state of atrocity
I still haven't found
The feeling I yearn for
But if I continue this battle
I will lose the war

"A Letter to the Dead (Dear Dad Pt. I)"

Dear Dad
It's your oldest son Joel
Just a word
From me to your soul
I wish I understood
Why you had to leave me
No one on this earth
Could take the place of my daddy

Life is so lonely
Now that you're gone
No one could change
That father son bond
I have no one to turn to
But the heavens above
The only place where I feel

There is still love

No one to teach me
The manly things I should know
But I know through spirit
You'll help me grow
I know you're in
A better place
Life is easier
For you to embrace

I can't wait
Until I see you again
You've been my father
But also my friend
You weren't perfect
But you tried your best
You went without
So I could have the best

I love you dad
No matter how far
You'll always have
A place in my heart
No one could take
All the good times we had
Cause you'll always be

My number one dad

"Friends Forever"

I never thought there'd be a time
Where I had to say goodbye
So many laughs
And now I'm left to cry
Leaving everyone I love
In the opposite direction
Knowing I'll never find
This kind of affection

The friends I've made
And do anything for
I'm walking away
And closing the door
And as I start to walk away
I begin to cry
I'm leaving the place I love
And I don't even know why

I never dreamed
That this day would come
When the life of my best friends
Would eventually be done

I set to walk a different path
Taking me way off track
But sometimes I wish
I could go back

I didn't know the love I had
Until I left it behind
The bonds that formed
Were one of a kind
And now that I'm gone
I see how much they cared
How lucky I am
To have friends this rare

As I go my separate way
I'll never forget
The friends I had
And the first times we met
I'll always remember
The times we spent together
And even though I'm far away
We'll be friends forever

"The Cage Where Light Shines Through"

Just a young man

Lost in his own ways
Biting back on anger
Has shown through on these dark days
No different than you and I
Except he is surrounded by concrete
With no place to turn
He gives up in defeat

He writes out his life
As he reflects on the past
As bright as the walls he looked upon
He is an outcast
As if life hadn't already
Lead him to a dead end road
A six by six cell
Reveals all that is unknown

There used to be so much
For him to explore
Now he waits for death
To come knocking on his door
He's lost it all
Family and even friends
Sitting alone in prison
Leaves him wishing it all would end

Realizing defeat

He now has open eyes
To an aspect of life
He never could recognize
With nowhere to look
But a blanket of blue in the sky
He begins to pray
For a new type of life

He begins to learn
Things he never did before
That no matter what the sin
God was still knocking on his door
And even though prison
Isn't where he wants to be
He wouldn't change a thing
Cause he'd still be like me

"Blood On My Hands"

In the dark I slowly walk
Down the beach, under a pier
Falling to my knees
I feel serenity when I'm here
I look up to the moon
With my hands laid out
Covered in the blood of another

I hold a heart with doubt

My instinct to survive
Has taught me to flee
But this heart is distinct
For it holds a love for me
It possess' understanding
For the way I choose to live
I fear this foreign deity
But it has so much to give

My selfishness gives me power
To easily destroy this heart
But I seem to feel an emotion
That won't let me break it apart
I concentrate on the beat
As it pulsates in my hand
Blood slips through my fingers
Falling to the sand

I feel the urge to toss it
In the deepest part of the ocean
But I can't bring myself to do it
With this newly acquired emotion
I don't wanna drain the blood
Of its very last drop
Don't wanna make it grow

If I can never make it stop

But this heart feeds my soul
Without taking a bite
Lost in my mind
I can't decide what is right
I don't wanna let it die
Or be the one that kills it
As our hearts become connected
I'll be the one that feels it

"Angel of Mine"

Sometimes it seems like
The words never come out right
And no matter what I do
It gets harder the more I try
Like a rose that grows
From the concrete ground
Lost in a lonely world
Yet you made me feel found

I don't know how you do
The things you do
Filled with love and kindness
Makes a beautiful you

Like an angel of God
You shine light on my soul
Broken apart by life
Yet you made me feel whole

How does one be blessed
As he knows he doesn't deserve it
Not knowing what he did
To receive something so perfect
Surely God has smiled on me
As I've been blessed with a curse
For you are my biggest fear
Yet you see the best of me as my worst

If I could paint you a picture
To show you how I feel
I'd want to convey just one message
As you would know that it was real
I'm not the first
And certainly not the last
I just hope I'm not another guy
Who came and passed

I'm certainly not perfect
But I try to be for you
And I know I do things
That you wish I didn't do

But I promise that I'll always
Be here for you
No matter what happens
We'll always make it through

"Comfortably Numb"

I don't understand
Why I'm living life this way
I have all the words
I just don't know what to say
The road less traveled
Searching for nothing
But knowing in the end
There has to be something

Living so comfortable
But only in the dark
Life is easier
Though it doesn't seem smart
Fear of failure
Leaves me content
Not going backwards
But forward progress is the intent

Where is my vision

The key to my future
I've lost focus on reality
A magic like wisher
So it seems like my demise
Is the easiest way to play
No need to worry
If tomorrow is an extinct day

If the night falls on me
Leaving me to pieces
The drama of tomorrow
Breaks worries and decreases
For at times I wish
I could be something or someone
Plagued by myself
I'm just comfortably numb

"Killing Osiris, Killing Me"

You showed me a love
Something I hated
Feelings of emotion
That you created
I was fully protected
From any type of pain
By keeping myself

Out of the rain

Then you built me up
So the fall would be rough
So much in love
I could no longer be tough
You thawed out a heart
That was never to be used
Being naïve at closing
Left me in love and abused

How did I let this
Get so far
I walked myself
Straight into the dark
Knowing very well
What you can't see gets under your feet
And letting your guard down
Can leave you in defeat

Betraying our love
Breaks my heart in two
But betraying your best friend
Tears the rest of me through
I never thought this pain
Could actually exist
From something as simple

As the loss of a kiss

Your evil ways remind me
Of a murderer, Seth
An Egyptian god
Bringing his brother to death
You too have drown me
In the Nile of betrayal
Scatter the pieces of my heart
But don't leave a trail

"Ghost"

I am the one that you think of
Before you sleep
The one that haunts your dreams
Causing you to awake and weep
I am the one in which
You fear the most
You've been sleeping with the enemy
My love is a ghost

I am the one that holds
Your beating heart
As it lies in my hands
I will surely leave my mark

For I am cursed with evil
As I lurk
I decide our future
And how much it's worth

I am the one
Known to many as a devil
No love is good enough
None at which meet my level
I am the one
That will rarely come out of disguise
For you speak of my evil
Yet I see the selfish intent in your eyes

Yes, I am the one
That fights human emotion
For I faithfully admit
I fear of drowning in your ocean
Every moment spent
Will be a memory in your mind
But perhaps one day
I'll find a real love to be mine

"Venomous"

If I could find the words

To tell you how I feel
I'd say it like a dagger
Wounds scar but never heal
If you want I could show you
The break of it all
What salt feels like in the wound
You'd be amazed at what you saw

So you ask me why
Am I so cold like the midnight rain
And I won't lie
You chase the blood right out of my veins
So watch it trickle down
Can you see the color of my fears
Listen to the screams around
They look just like my tears

You thought all this time
I was the one slithering along
Waiting for a venomous bite
But I was never that strong
I wrapped myself around
Everything but your fingertips
I'd die to hear you say my name
I'd die to kiss your lips

"Don't Lean on Me"

Don't lean on me
I'm not that strong
I've been through too much
To carry on
I'm not build like rock
I'm not your stepping-stone
I wish I could be
But you're better off on your own

Don't lean on me
I will surely let you fall
You can't depend on me
I'll never hear your call
I'm stiff but not sturdy
I can barely keep myself together
Like loss of gravity
Things will never get better

Don't lean on me
Even my insides crumble
Emotions never get me far
So I keep myself humble
Don't fall for me
When I'm already falling
I could never pick you up

It's just not my calling

Don't lean on me
You will only get hurt
And if you fall in love
Things will only get worse
It's like hanging by a thread
How much do you trust
I'll disappear in the wind
Leaving your tears in my dust

"Ire (Part I) Your Pain"

If you say I run
Then cease from trying to catch me
I do so for a reason
I do not wish to be seen
For you do not know
What your oddities may bring unto you
Plague and troubles
Will see their way through

Though you say you proceed
In love and in tears
But I assure you now
I bring much more than fears

I'm a troubled man
With a fiery dark past
No person can love one
Who has traveled my path

If you dare to break the chains
And play with my fire
I warn you now a bitter feeling
Will become of you, Ire
If my wrath doesn't break you
It will scar you for life
Then you too will feel
Bloody pain without the knife

You do not want to feel
The inside of my heart
It no longer burns for love
It burns to be apart
But if you want to see things
As they once were as a whole
Travel through the fire
The key to life is thy soul

"Ire (Part II) My Pain"

Eyes do not lie

They are the window to my soul
Take a look into mine
And let the story be told
The beginning battle
That nearly left a baby unnourished
A plague of disease
That almost flourished

Silver and gold
Could not buy what one yearned
As you cross the bridges
That should have been burned
But the memories echo
As I reflect and ponder
My pain will stray from you
As if it were silent thunder

Recurring attacks
Set forth against my own kin
This time it is my leader
Lured in by sin
As I watch my own blood
Fall to the devil himself
To be given pain is one thing
But death was not to be dealt

As if torture were not suitable

For a family of simplicity
Agony must be fulfilled
Before thou can feel felicity
I've been beaten down
So with anger I've caught fire
To protect the remaining pieces
They now call Ire

"Blood on the Tip of a Paint Brush"

She's delicate like a flower
With one pedal left
Torn to pieces by love
That each thief has kept
She has shed her tears
And built herself back up
Solid as a rock
With untimely luck

She seems so strong
For a heart that's been abused
A quiet strength in her love
That has always been used
So why does she trust me
With the last piece of her heart
Only a fool would paint beauty

Using blood on her art

My hands are dirty
And bare the pain of broken love
They hold confusion and tears
Things I created thereof
I feel like a monster
As her head lies on my chest
Trusting me with her life
Even after all I've confessed

I admire her faith in a love
That has failed her so many times
But I don't understand her choosing
Of all the people she could find
Maybe it's the boldness
That glows through my art
Blood tells an honest story
Shining light on the dark

"One Step"

Falling away
Taking so many steps from you
The further I fall
The more hell I go through

As I make my choices
One bad leading to another
I don't wanna keep falling
But I feel like I'm being smothered

It seems like I'm unable
To pick myself back up
Get myself together
And stop screwing up
I can feel the flames
As my sin gets thicker
This life I've been living
Has me falling to hell quicker

I can feel it in the air
Time is closing in on me
I can't do this by myself
I know you are the key
I still hear that voice
In the back of my mind
Saying, "You can always come back
There is still time"

I know I'm not worthy
My whole life is full of sin
But a friend reminded me
You would still take me in

And a tear came to my eye
When I saw the last thing she said
No matter how far you fall
You can come back in one step

"The Perfect Drug"

My fears have broken through
Tearing at my insides
Like open wounds bleeding
Leading myself to die
I've consumed your love
More than I can handle
The feeling burns my heart
Like a melting candle

I don't want you to be a battle
That I always have to fight
I know that I'll lose
Cause you're my only light
I can't walk away
I feel like I'm stuck
But I lust for the feeling
Like you're some kind of drug

Sometimes I wonder

If it's even worth fighting for
But when I think about losing you
I only want more
I don't know why I sour myself
And pretend that I don't care
Cause inside I realize
My life is better with you there

You're the worst habit
That runs through my veins
Thickening like blood
So that I'm barred to you by chains
But I won't fight your burn
Because you're the purest cut
I need you in my life
You're the perfect drug

"In Your Arms"

Another day goes by
Just thinking about you
It gets harder with time
I don't know what to do
They say love grows stronger
When time sets you apart
Though it may be true

It's also tearing at my heart

Just another day
Without your smile
The days grow longer
And I know it's gonna be while
It's already starting
To tear at my heart
I can't take the miles
That keep us apart

But I'm learning something
As the days pass by
That without your love
I don't think I could survive
You've become something
Like apart of me
My heart's always been locked
But you ended up with the key

You're the only one
That brings a light to my eyes
The one that makes me happy
And worth living my life
Cause I miss you more
Each and every day
And I love you more

Than I could ever say

Forever doesn't seem
Like it's quite long enough
To share our lives together
And to show you my love
I'll forever be yours
As we grow old like the stars
And when it's all over with
I wanna die lying in your arms

"The Portrait"

We had a relationship built
With a concrete foundation
And the combined strength of love
To get through any situation
Though we had our walls
To confront our sincerity
Like green vines we climbed over them
Showing prosperity

Looking back I can see
That wall covered with vines
For every one that made it over
Made us stronger in time

Even buds of rare flowers
Would bloom along the way
Showing why our love
Would be stronger than yesterday

I guess you saw our wall
In a portrait of its own
A beautiful disaster
Covering each and every stone
There was reason behind
Every brick that lay before us
But there was truth in the vines
That always restored us

When I look at this portrait
I see art embracing such love
Though every brush stroke wasn't perfect
The picture was enough
It tells a story of us
And exhibits strength and truth
But I guess you couldn't see the beauty
In the disaster we pursued

I framed this memory
And nailed it to the wall I see most
Giving me strength when I feel far
Though I'm actually close

Moving on I've taken the lesson
But I'll never know why
You traded a beautiful disaster in
For a perfect lie

"Angels Screw Up Too"

Innocence runs deep
In this angel of mine
But the feelings she had
Would change in time
Her touch runs deep
Through the tissue of my skin
But I never thought
She'd be the one to do me in

She picked me up
Off of solid ground
She whispered, I love you
In a believable sound
When all was wrong
I found comfort in her power
But the deeper I dug
The more she grew sour

I've never been

Too fond of heights
But I let her carry me away
To a different part of life
One that I never saw
Nor wanted to be apart of
What I feared from the beginning
I saw that it was love

I felt safe with the angel
That made me feel this way
But I should have known
It would come to this day
I made myself vulnerable
To something I thought was pure
But in the end
You can never be so sure

The love of an angel
Will always make you smile
But remember it only lasts
For a little while
And the day will come
When she betrays you
But don't cry for a second
Because angels screw up too

"Giving Up On Me"

You said it a million times
That I was the only one for you
And how it would take forever
To find somebody new
You're moving on
And you can't even look at me
What happened to your faith
That we were meant to be

If I was so great
Why'd you leave me here to rot
You left me so lonely
With all the words you forgot
I survived my thoughts
Believing in your faith
Nothing else mattered
When I seen your face

You said it a million times
That you'd never give up on me
You'd spend your whole life
Trying to make me see
That all the happiness
Could belong to us
Though I was scared

Deep inside, I gave you my trust

It was so easy to believe
And just as easy to give up
You left me here lonely
With all the words you forgot
I put up walls
To see if you cared to break them down
We had everything we wanted
Why did you give up now

"The Kind of Pain Called Suicide"

I used to wonder
Why anyone would want to die
Nothing could possibly
Be that bad about life
Everyone can find
Something to live for
Nothing is worth dying
You just need something more

I always thought
Suicide was an easy way out
I never understood
What that person must be thinking about

Until I felt the pain
That makes everything go away
You don't think of anything
And you never know what to say

When your mind is filled with hurt
And your heart with pain
It doesn't seem possible
That this feeling will go way
Your heart feels tight
And it gets harder to breathe
Your hands sometimes shake
When you realize it wasn't meant to be

When you lose love
And a best friend in a day
You feel so alone
Like a lost, wandering stray
Nothing seems worthy
Of living anymore
There are no brighter days
When someone closes the door

The world is cruel
And it seems there's no way out
You'd only understand
If you knew what pain was about

When you lose love forever
You can feel it inside
Now I understand
The kind of pain called suicide

"Running with the Wild"

One mans cry
Trying to reach the wild
To roam the jungle
On my own secret isle
Escaping industrialization
To be apart of nature
Enjoying life for what it is
As my permanent fixture

Lord of the jungle
If I could ask of ye
Morph myself
Into a creature of the sea
So then I could swim
In a blissful state
No worries on my mind
No destiny, no fate

Or a beast of the land

Roaming the jungle as I please
Humans are defected
We are creatures of disease
As a wild animal of the land
I could be the real me
The world through my eyes
Is not close to what you see

I question my life
As if God made a mistake
To be in this body
Feels like I'm out of my fate
It's all in my mind
I just want to be free
Living the life of the wild
Will be my legacy

If only I could run
And get away from all this
The chance at being free
Has to exist
If I could convince God
To change me as a child
I'd still be me
But I'd be running with the wild

"The Man After Me"

I hope it's easier
To talk to him
And that he is the man
I have never been
I saw this day coming
Just not this way
We said friends forever
Even though I pushed you away

I hope his kiss
Tastes as good as mine
Though I was never sweet
What was that feeling in your spine
If you must forget
In order to move on
I hope the memories fade
When your feelings are gone

If the memories don't fade
Then the feelings never left
You can fool your body
But your heart is not deaf
It hears your soul
Crying out for something more
Don't lie to yourself

By closing the door

When you make love
I hope it's not our way
If it is even love
Or just sexual play
But I hope he can do
Everything I did and more
Isn't that why you're moving on
To find something more pure

But most of all
I hope you never think of me
Every time you kiss
Don't let your heart skip a beat
I'll always be there
But like the rest you'll push me out
I hope you love again
And I never cause you doubt

"Betrayed by Blood"

What is loyalty
As it is between two men being brothers
As one fades away
While the other abides with the mother

Is family not a priority
Nor his teaching of values in life
For I would not be surprised
If this man brought to be a knife

Flesh is flesh,
Inconveniently we are blood
Not drawn together by heart
For he has darkened his love
Creator of all says love thou family
But this has made me afraid
Turning your back on your blood
I tell you now I feel betrayed

If you do not see the fire
That burns through my eyes
Guilt should rest on you
As you feel the flames of my despise
You have entrapped yourself
In a world of selfish intent
Do you not see the benefits of the world
Will leave you in torment

For what could have been
Had you chosen the brighter path
Greed will help you
As you construct your own wrath

You are my blood
I can see through all the lies
I just pray to God
It doesn't lead to your demise

"The Death of a King"

The greatest gift
Not only from above
But sent to earth
To show his love
Descending as a king
None of which suffer his reality
That one of such highness
Would meet such a fatality

No other would love
And be more of a friend
For who else would sacrifice
Their life for your sins
To be physically tortured
Nearly beaten to death
Saying, "Father forgive them"
Under his very last breath

How does one love

Such a human breed
As our lives are based on
Temptation and greed
Our sinful habits
Reflect my fathers' cause
Mirroring the future
Knowing all of our flaws

Yet with love and passion
He still chose to die
For the sins of the world
And for you and I
Not because he had to
But to save us from ourselves
The blood of the lamb
Our greatest wealth

"An Aspect of Life"

Nothing is satisfying
Where is my joy
Nothing is comforting
Like a lost little boy
Everything is plain
Life's colors are dull
I wanna be at the edge of the earth

Ready to fall

This world isn't for me
I think God made a mistake
My heart grows more empty
Every new day I wake
Everywhere I look
It's all just the same
Different pictures
With the same old frame

What am I looking for
That I can't seem to get
If I seek out this mystery
Will the puzzle piece fit
Would it even matter
If the picture is just as plain
As the world I live in
I can't seem to escape this rain

How do you live life
When the grass is dull green
And the sky is the same
A boring blue and white scene
The birds are just black
And the squirrels don't even move
Oh Lord, I need you

I just don't know what to do

It may seem like
I should be held in contempt
But I do hold a curiosity
That I wish to make content
There's gotta be more
To life than this
Show me something brighter
A Heavenly type bliss

"A Thirst for Seduction (The Curse)"

Seduction falls
In the eye of the beholder
But the sensation you feel
Could not be colder
Heightened arousal
Explicitly made aware
But the love for one another
Is never there

His fingers are cold
As they crawl like a spider on your skin
A diminutive feeling of fear
Starts to surface from within

As his hand touches your face
You feel his years of sadness
And when you look into his eyes
You see a lifetime of loneliness

You feel a sudden sense of sympathy
For a darkened man
But as you flea to be with the wolf
You quickly become the lamb
As you touch his body
He licks his lips like a snake
Not knowing what to expect
The excitement over takes

You close your eyes
And feel his breath on your neck
As he makes you feel in love
Yet afraid of meeting death
Like a vampire you can feel his teeth
Sink into your skin
Orgasmic feelings down your spine
As your arms have become pinned

Questions of his intent
Surface as you endure in your lust
Fear never felt so delighting
Along with the absence of trust

Under his control
You can no longer move yourself
As his tongue swims in your mouth
You wouldn't dream of anything else

Loss of control as a mental element
Has you thirsting for more
But he sees you so purely
Not his kind, which he adores
Your fear does not make you afraid
Nor your lust make you thirst
Your thirst is afraid
That your lust for fear will never be satisfied
…The curse

"Release"

Standing on the edge
Dreaming of a memory
Remembering a spark of love
That once lived in me

The sun that once arose
Upon my heart to shine
Stormed on my heart
Before I could make you mine

All was lost
A broken heart buried in confusion
A shining from the dark side
Became a twisted illusion

As I resume to the darkness
I cry unto the sky
Looking up at God
Only asking, "Why"

Will anyone pick up
The pieces of a broken soul
Warm the outer body
My heart seems to be cold

Although time has mended
The tears of a broken heart
Ones own mind
Does not know of a start

A cold and bitter heart
Leads me to darkness
The rest of my body
Only knows loneliness

Will forever alone
Be the fate of my heart

Death upon my flesh
As the rest falls apart

Or will a new moon shine
And set forth my peace
Resurrection to my heart
And my soul to be released

"Alive"

Rest assure
i'll put your mind at ease
Emotions formed by you
developed into a disease
Sorry never cut it
but I promise I don't hate you
Except for the days
i think about what you put me through
Never thought your memory
would last this long
Took you and your lies
to see I'm not really that strong
Mirror my emotions
that were cut by your lies
Enemies never hurt me
like you did inside

No one, no one
can say with pride
Tears in my eyes
never made me feel more alive

Roads are broken
where they used to be paved
Apologies accepted
but I can never be saved
Now won't you leave
and take your memories along
Could the memories leave
and really be gone
Open the door
and softly say goodbye
Remember us
but don't pretend to cry

"Leaving the Body"

For years I've been looking
At the world through my eyes
Everything looks bigger
When you take it all inside
I've painted my own picture
Adding things as I please

Attempts to add beauty
To make life more colorful than the one I lead

To feel complete
What all would need to fill the paper
Watching the second hand move slowly
I guess I'll tend to it later
Seconds turn to minutes
As the hours turn into shorter days
Several chapters into life
And I still haven't found the way

I look deeper into the white sheet
Past the red and blue paint
It turns brown and comes to life
Revealing this creatures fate
For only one purpose
It came to me to do with it as I will
My purpose is filled with selection
Unlike this creature of the still

A new outlook upon myself
I now look from the outside
Sitting on the edge of a star
I've left my body without a mind
I look at the temple I've been given
To live a few short years

Caught up in human vision
I now see I'd much rather be here

"Code of Ethics"

I will dream what others fear
And live to be afraid
I will pursue my fantasies
Despite what people say

I will give everything I have
Until my very last breath
In love and in life
I will give 100% until my death

I will turn fear into ambition
For it will not defeat me
Because everyone knows
Nothing worth having comes easy

I will lend a hand to the priest
Who might slip and fall
But I will sacrifice my body
For the one who wishes not to live at all

I will always be aware

Of the mirror I possess
I could be a hero to a child
Who copies all that I suggest

I will slow my clock
To recognize others in pain
Take time to be their sun
Even if I have to walk with them in the rain

I will see the good in the bad
And know that God has a plan
I will have faith in his wisdom
And know that I am just a man

I will minimize my human nature
And shun away from sin
I will strive for perfection
The way Jesus has always been

I will acknowledge my body
Is just a temple that will die
And at Heaven's Gates I will be proud
To say I lived this life

"The Last Piece of My Heart"

Dear God,
I have a question for you
Can you see how much pain
You're putting me through
Do you see the tears I shed
Every time someone dies
Yet you keep taking them away
Despite how much I cry

Why do you want me
To be here all alone
You took all of my grandparents
Before I could know
What they were like
And if they would have loved me
And then you go ahead
And take away the one that made me

I was only fifteen
I wasn't ready for that
How strong do you think I am
That you think I don't need a dad
And now I've got friends
That are taking their own life
God, how many times

Do you want me to cry

The sad thing is
It all happened before I was nineteen
And the family I have left
Has already left me
Just me and my mom
I'm just waiting for the day
When you see the last piece of my heart
And take it away

"Take Me Back"

I remember all the times
We had together
And I thought the party
Would last forever
All the drinks and laughs
I'd never forget
And every drunken moment
I'd never regret

Partyin' all night
Til' the sun came up
And when the cops were comin'
We had nothing but love

We had a case of Keylight
For the week day nights
And a keg on the weekends
To keep us going all night

I fell in love with the party
Never thought I'd have to leave
The thought of it ending
I just couldn't believe
And now that it's here
I'm forced to walk away
I guess there comes a time
When we must go our separate ways

Take me back
To freshmen year
When we actually split
One case of beer
Take me back
So I can do it all again
I'd do it 10 more times
As long as it was with my friends

Put your drinks in the air
To remember the times
The good and the bad
Take some time to rewind

For these were the best days
For our group of friends
And if we had a choice
We'd do it all over again

"There Goes My Life"

I woke up one day
Seeing my life for what it is
A striking image
Of what everyone says
I'm everything and nothing
Of what I wanted to be
I've locked myself in failure
And I can't set myself free

Whatever happened
To the dreams I used to have
No plans, no worries
Faith and hope is all I had
Now I have nothing
With no sense of direction
All alone
With no feelings of affection

They say you only have

One life to live
So far I've wasted mine
With too many sins to forgive
If I ever make it to heaven
I'll be lucky to make it in
Cause I've ruined my life
With the places I've been

I have no future
Only days to pass me by
This whole time I couldn't see
My own life flying by
And now that I see
It's already gone
There goes my life
Where did I go wrong

"The Beast"

The creator of my seed
Has shown to be a beast
A monster, but blind
For he doesn't remember me
In the light he is my father
Sheltering me with care
In the dark he meets with Satan

With an empty bottle
They have shared

This bottle possess' him
With anger and rage
Observing his monstrosities
They throw him in a cage
Upon his release
He falls back into the dark
A full moon and moonshine
Has blackened his heart

I defend our queen
But not without a fight
His power comes from a source
That blinds him from what is right
Throwing me to the ground
His strength exceeds my own
Pulling blades on his allies
The demons have shown

Betrayal of my family
Will never exist
But I love him so I pray
That everything be fixed
As the sun begins to rise
The beast finally sleeps

I'll pray he doesn't wake
So for awhile there is peace

"Never Escape"

Everyday I'm alive
I fight for a breath
There's temptation in the ease
That comes along with death
I'm tired of fighting
So tired of the struggle
I've worn out my welcome
Indulging in such trouble

I fight each battle
Not recognizing it's a war
Torn to pieces inside
What am I fighting for
I can't answer the question
That should be keeping me alive
Can't find a reason to live
When I'm empty inside

My fight with agony
Has drained the last drop
Knocked down by its lack of sympathy

There's no will to get back up
I don't even have the strength
To crawl into safety
Life has had its way
As it stripped and raped me

I don't even feel the pain
My body has become numb
A slit to the wrist
Would be painful for some
But life is more cruel
There's no trickery to fool it
Unable to escape the rain
That has showered me with bullets

"The Rules of Emotion"

You ask for the words
That are bottled up inside
What makes up a hollow man
Who has nothing else to hide
The truth is I'm filled to the top
With every emotion you can feel
But words can't describe them
To show you they are real

My kind has been taught
That you cannot reveal your scars
A sign of weakness
Will show what you really are
The pieces of my broken heart
Are cutting me every day
If I shed a single tear
They just say I'll be okay

They tear down emotion
Like it's a devil in disguise
Shoving it back inside
But it resurfaces in my eyes
I'm quiet with my rage
Silent with my fears
Spilling emotion like water
But nobody wants to hear

I'm not proud of my scars
But they made me who I am
As hard as I try to describe it
I don't think I can
You ask for the words
To explain a misshapen heart
But I'm not supposed to say
Or else you'll think I'm falling apart

They tell me they care
But they rarely ever show it
I've been dying inside
And nobody even knows it
It's ironic that this paper
Is the only thing that knows my heart
The tree that it used to be
Had to die to be my art

"Die With You (Dear Dad Pt. II)"

Dear Dad, it's been 8 years
Since the last time I wrote you
The feelings never show
So nobody knows what I go through
It's kinda hard
With you not around
I wonder how you feel
When you're looking down

I would never wish
For you to come back
I cry like I would but
I wouldn't want you to see me like that
The world is cruel
Don't want you to relive the pain

Even though your death
Has become my rain

A silent killer
But I know you see my broken heart
Pray for me as I pray for you
So I can stray from the dark
I've taken on your demons
I know you see my troubles
I just wish I could be with you
And be free from the struggle

Last night I saw you standing
With Jesus by your side
Surrounded by beauty
Was the garden that gave you life
I dreamed you were a bird
So free, I envied the way you flew
Forgive me, but sometimes
I wish I would have just died with you

"Too Far Gone"

I dance alone on this boulevard
Of broken dreams
All my faults

Lead to my guilty screams
I'm on a path of self-destruction
When will it end
Killing myself
And losing all of my friends

I see my life
Being flushed away
The depth of my addiction
Shadows my today
Helpless and powerless
Where do I turn
They say I'm only 12 steps away
To avoid the burn

My bridge of will power
To get me over this
Has collapsed into pieces
The more I try to resist
I've lost my grip
On ideas that I had control
I'm fighting my flesh
Just to save my soul

This mental obsession
Lusts for the poison I love
They care about me

So it's them I'm thinking of
Lack of understanding
Will leave me in a battle alone
Please don't give up on me
When it seems I'm too far gone

"Still in My Heart"

It's been a long time
But you're still in my heart
I thought I had finished
When I didn't even start
I thought I could forget
And make these feelings go away
Now I see myself down the road
Feeling the same way

No matter what I do
I can never seem to get over you
I try so hard
But it's not what my heart wants to do
So I shut you out
And hide you from myself
Hoping to let go
But it doesn't seem to help

When I see you I want you
When I think of you I need you
And my only wish was
That you'd feel the same way too
I can still remember
Your beautiful smile
If only I could of made it
Last a little while

All that I want
Is to hold you tight
A small secret spark
To rekindle the light
I wish I could turn back
The hands of time
And feel the love again
When you were mine

Everyday that I breathe
I pray that you'll come back to me
They say it's not likely
But it's through faith I can see
Like all of creation
And everything that is
It's through faith I live
And know love exists

"Sapphire Diamond"

Your beauty runs deep
Like the ocean water
Surely created
In the image of our father
Heaven sent
By God himself
One of his finest arts
Greater than all else

Your eyes sparkle
Like a sapphire diamond
So rare and exquisite
No other could find one
And your skin is sleek
Like ancient roman silk
Only kings could experience
How true beauty felt

How lucky am I
To possess such treasure
Your unconditional love
In which no one could measure
And the love I feel
For a queen on high
Shall flow like the Nile

And never run dry

"Shangri-La"

Let's escalade toward the heavens
To see what it's like
Taste the particles of the galaxy
In a brand new light
And then we can stop
And take a walk on mars
To see what it's like
To sleep under blue stars

As we walk on the crest
Our shadows reflect green
My breath looks purple
But it doesn't bother me
Let's slew onto a gold ring
And ice skate for the night
If its motion goes left
Then we'll go right

Flip the switch
And turn gravity off
Be amazed by a change
And don't ever stop

I feel weightless
Floating above this dream
This Elysian experience
Is my kind of scheme

I am freer than a bird
Who flies in an earthly sky
Freer then a newborn
Who has nothing on its mind
I'm so close to Heaven
It feels like Shangri-La
So peaceful and beautiful
No earthly flaws

"Deeper Waters"

I've walked myself
From the shallow end to the deep
Curious to see how far I can go
Without losing my feet
I have felt the pressure
With the water pressed against my chest
But with confidence I keep going
Putting this curiosity to rest

I may have taken

More than I can swallow
With the troubles I've received
And with more to follow
I can taste a stream of water
Flowing into my mouth
But not quite enough
For me to want out

With human intentions
I keep walking with the blind
Swimming with the sinners
With the same intention in mind
But I'm starting to think
I'm on a fool's quest for gold
In the end could I end up
Losing my own soul

"If I'm Losing You"

Sometimes I can't find the words
To explain how I feel
Because it goes so deep
And it feels too real
Let me open up my heart
With the words that I write
As I let you in my dark

And shine a little light

You're not even gone
But I can feel the pain
Right now you're my sunshine
But I can already feel the rain
And all the time
It makes me wonder why
If we have to leave each other
Then why did we ever try

I don't exactly know
Why this is my biggest fear
I just look up to heaven
With an eye full of tears
Cause if I'm losing you
Then I'm losing me
They say life goes on
But I just can't see

No one knows my fears
Cause I always tend to hide it
And the tears that I shed
I always try to fight it
But somehow I know
The reality of our fate
I just wish I could convince God

Before it's too late

I don't know if I can say
Goodbye today
Because tomorrow I know
You'll still be far away
So if I'm losing you
I'll hold you close as long as I can
Cause I know that if I keep you
I'll be a better man

"Guilt"

I just can't seem
To get it out of my head
Over and over
I hear the words you said
"I don't understand
Why you hurt me the way you do
I can't understand
I thought I was so good to you"

A tear almost runs
From the corner of my eye
When I feel the shame
Inside I want to die

I feel broken hearted
I know I've let you down
You had so much faith in me
And I never came around

She's an earthly angel
A blessing in disguise
I can see it so clearly
When I look into her eyes
After all the pain I've caused
And the things I've put her through
With a tear in her eye
She says, "I still love you"

It kills me inside
To know you feel this way
But you still forgive
And love me anyway
You're so good to me
Even though I don't deserve it
And I never do anything
That's worthy of earning it

I pray every night
The Lord would let me fix my past
To gain your trust again
So this shame would pass

The guilt builds heavier
Every time I look at you
And I shed a tear
Every time you say, "I still love you"

"In the Corner of my Mind"

For some strange reason
I'm throwing it all away
It seems like the right choice
If only for today
And I know someday
That I might regret it
But I know one thing
I'll never forget it

As of late
I tend to have these dreams
Where I finally realize
That I'm struggling to breathe
I'm walking in the dark
And it hurts to admit
That I knew all along
This is the feeling I'd regret

I guess sometimes

It's not always what you want
Some things belong
Not to be undone
But how can you know
When you choose in love
It feels so right
But you hate what you've done

In the corner of my mind
There's a battle of what is right
I could never decide
With this vicious fight
Maybe it was wrong
And it blinded me in the end
But what if it was right
And it would only happen again

"Just Wanted You to Know"

They say the holidays are a time
For giving to others
To love your family
And treat enemies like brothers
And yet all I've been able
To give you is pain
Tear after tear

Falling down like rain

It hurts me to see
The sadness in your heart
And even though I'm gone
I don't wanna see you fall apart
You deserve so much more
And I hope someday you'll see
That you'll find better love
Than you ever found in me

You may never understand
Why I do the things I do
But if you know one thing
Know it was because I loved you
I wanted better for you
And the life you had ahead
But I knew if I was in it
It would be something you'd regret

I'm poison to your heart
And in the end you'd suffer
So to avoid this pain
I must give you to another
I could never make you happy
So I had to let you go
You were too perfect for me

I just wanted you to know

"You're Welcome"

Do you see the way she smiles
At all the little things
The way she mixes up her words
But you still know what she means
Can you see it in her eyes
When she's right where she wants to be
Yes I know
Cause she once belonged to me

Do you feel her cuddle up
Next to you in bed
The way she always remembers
Everything you've said
Can you feel the way she loves
With all of her heart
Can you feel just how lucky
How lucky you are

Do you hear all her pain
In the cracks of her voice
The way it feels like a knife
When you have no choice

Can you hear her letting go
Of all her fears to be with you
Yes I know
Cause I used to be the one she ran to

Do you know if I hadn't made the mistake
Of leaving her behind
That she would still be with me
And her heart would still be mine
I know that you are thankful
So I'll say to you, you're welcome
Just don't ever leave her
Or you'll regret it when you're gone

"Better To Not Know"

Now that I'm alone
All I wanna do is die
And it would be alright
If God took my life
Cause I don't really need
To find someone else
And I don't really need
Anybody's help

I'm not okay

I need to shut down
The loneliness is killing me
More than not having you around
I could hate you forever
For bringing us together
But knowing this feeling
Made me feel better

I never even knew
That all my life I've been alone
I never felt better
To have a heart of stone
But you broke it away
Making me a new man
Temporarily for the better
But in the end I've been damned

I knew all along
In the end I'd get hurt
But I opened my trust
Only to get stomped into the dirt
I can protect myself
From getting hurt by love
But I can never go back
To not knowing what it was

"If You See my Reflection"

After years of memories
When you still think of me
My face will start to fade
The more years you come to see
Everything will be better
You'll find what you deserve
True happiness in your heart
To show you what you're worth

But if you see my reflection
As the snow hits the ground
If the ice on your window
Reflects my face with a frown
You should know it's me
Still melted by your love
Looking over you
Like it should have been us

Though time has probably mended
All the pieces of your heart
I know I was the reason
And I was the biggest part
But I will live to see
Your heart reemerge
With someone who deserves it

And won't let you hurt

But if you see my reflection
As the spring rain falls down the trees
You might see a grin
Knowing you still think of me
But after all this time
I know I will only be
A scar from your past
And a reflection in your memory

"A Recognizable Death"

How would you feel
On the day that I die
Knowing I won't be around
While your still alive
Could you look at me
The body I used to live in
Now without life
Can you see me in that coffin

How would you feel
Would a tear come to your eye
Or would you grieve with anger
And let it build up inside

Would you blame God
For taking me away
Would you even care
Cause my death could be today

What if I took my own life
Would it make you think again
About our relationship
And if you were a friend
What would you think about
If it might be your fault
And what if it was
Would it bother you at all

No one takes the time
To recognize death
The spirit may live on
But this is temporary flesh
Suicide or homicide
Death is all the same
As I move on
I'll let you decide who to blame

"Heart & Soul vs. Flesh & Mind"

I love the Heavens

But the my body loves sin
On my deathbed I'll pray
That he knows my heart and lets me in
I swear I never meant
To turn out this way
Hear me Lord
And the words that I say

Dive into my heart
And you will see
That the evil that lurks
Does not live inside of me
My flesh has gained strength
From the mistakes I've made
And inside my heart
It is I that I hate

My mind works in fashion
With the devils thoughts
He plants ideas
For my flesh to sought
I empower my enemy
With each sin I complete
But deep in my heart
The Lord is who I seek

I pray for the day

When I take my final breath
That the Lord will forgive me
And take my soul upon my death
To sit me by his side
And know my heart's true desire
For my flesh does not care
But to send my soul to fire

"Remind Me"

Remind me again
Of what I can't have
Say to me now
Come away from all that
Cause I still have big dreams
That just won't leave
So much in life
That I want to achieve

I cannot find peace
Nothing satisfies my soul
Except for my dreams
They fill the empty holes
Only when I sleep
Do I come close to my desires
The feeling of greatness

Takes me so much higher

I sleep in the clouds
With sunshine on my mind
Birds sing a song
In a land that does not know time
The sky is blue
But sometimes it's green
The impossible is nothing
Of what it sometimes seems

But the world is real
And things can't always be
The things I want
Can't always be seen
So somebody please remind me
Before I wake up and scream
That a dream is a dream
It can't always be

"Screaming Scars & Whispering Tears"

It's pain leaving the body
In a twisted sort of way
It's expression, a voice
When the words don't exist to say

Like an unparalleled tattoo
It's a scar with meaning
But like a bullet wound
It shows all that you are not seeing

It's a cry in a world
That rejects his tears
A release from the anxieties
He feels from his fears
The addiction spreads
Like a fatal disease
Once the blood spills
It brings him to his knees

Praying to a God
He never thought could exist
But seeking a life
That is better than his
He screams inside his head
With demons stitched into his soul
"Save me! I'm broken
I've lost all control"

Who could understand
Such an act of atrocity
Maybe I'm crazy
To elicit such curiosity

If a tear falls from a lonely eye
But no one's around to see it
Does it trickle down in vein
Since no one cared to hear it

"Rancor"

Freedom never felt
so good inside
Underneath
this broken heart of mine
Concentrating on
the things you said
Kill me inside
but confuse my head

You tricked me
with lies and deceit
Or maybe it's my fault
you got that close to me
Unless you can erase
a memory or two
I've only got one thing
to say to you

How could you leave me

here to die
And you thought
it was only a lie
Take a look at the damage
that you've done
Each lie unraveled
and came undone

Yes I tore down
my entire wall
Only because I thought
you'd catch me if I fall
Under your bridge of pain
i've been through
And now I only feel
one way for you

"My Suicide Note"

If I had it my way
No one would know
Just like all of the feelings
I never show
The ink on this paper
Will be my final piece of art
The only beauty I create

Is the result of my broken heart

Let there be no guilt
Or blame to cast
For the wall I projected
Was actually glass
I've been broken for years
The pieces just kept getting smaller
Don't blame the girl
It was my fault I loved her

It was my fault I left
It's my fault I'm alone
She's moved on but it's my fault
My love has grown
Because of the sharp pieces
I've pushed everyone away
To protect them from me
And the tears I've made

How do you care
For a handful of shattered glass
Too fragile, yet too dangerous
To think anything could last
Tears of pain run
Like a stream into a pool of blood
The result of anyone

That attempted to give me their love

It is known to all
That you cannot change the person you are
I can't erase the past
I can't take away the scars
But I can take away the pain
By eliminating the knife
I'll never hurt you again
This is my goodbye to life

Lightning Source UK Ltd.
Milton Keynes UK
UKHW011159060821
388387UK00001B/133